21st CENTURY LIVES
FOOTBALLERS

Liz Gogerly

WAYLAND

First published in 2007 by Wayland
Reprinted in 2007, 2008 and 2009

Copyright © Wayland 2007

Editor: Hayley Fairhead
Design: Proof Books

Wayland
338 Euston Road
London NW1 3BH

Wayland
Level 17/207 Kent Street
Sydney, NSW 2000

 Gogerly, Liz
   Footballers. - (21st century lives)
   1. Soccer players - Biography - Juvenile literature
   I. Title
   796.3'34'0922

ISBN 978-0-7502-5043-6

Printed in China

Wayland is a division of Hachette Children's Books,
an Hachette UK Company
www.hachette.co.uk

Cover: Thierry Henry in action.

Picture acknowledgements: Daniel Dal Zennaro/epa/Corbis: cover and
15, Empics/Topfoto: 1, David Klein/Professional Sport/Topfoto: 4,
Empics/Topfoto: 5, David Klein/Professional Sport/Topfoto: 6, Tommy
Hindley/Professional Sport/Topfoto: 7, Empics/Topfoto: 8, David
Klein/Professional Sport/Topfoto: 9, Empics/Topfoto: 10, 11, 12, 13,
David Klein/Professional Sport/Topfoto: 14, David Klein/Professional
Sport/Topfoto: 16, 17, Empics/Topfoto: 18, 19, David Klein/Professional
Sport/Topfoto: 20, 21.

Contents

Some definitions:

FIFA: The Fédération Internationale de Football Association

FIFPro: The Fédération International des Footballeurs Professionels

FWA: The Football Writers' Association

PFA: The Professional Footballers' Association

UEFA: The Union of European Football Associations

John Terry
The Rock

Terry does his stretches during a match against Manchester United in 2006.

> **"Stepping on to that football pitch, there's just a different person in me. I'd do anything in my power to help me and my team-mates win."**
>
> John Terry
> observer.guardian.co.uk

Name: John George Terry

Nickname: JT

Current club and number: Chelsea FC, 26

Position: Centre Back

Date and place of birth:
7 December 1980, Barking, London, England

First break: As a schoolboy Terry played for West Ham United schoolboys, Essex County and Sunday League Team, Senrab Football Club. When he left school in 1997 he was signed to Chelsea youth team where he played for the youth and reserve teams.

Brief history: Terry made his debut for Chelsea in 1998, becoming captain in 2003. From 1999 to 2000 he was on loan to Nottingham Forest. He made his debut for England in June 2003 and was chosen as captain of England in 2006, replacing David Beckham.

Major achievements: Being chosen as skipper for Chelsea and England. After an impressive 2004/05 season as captain of Chelsea he was voted Player of the Year by other professional players. Then, in 2006 he made the FIFA World Cup squad.

Something you might not know about him: As a trainee at Chelsea, Terry had to clean players Dennis Wise, Eddie Newton and David Lee's boots. He even had to vacuum and clean up the players' rooms at the club.

Become a pro!: As a defender you've got to stay solid and go in hard. You've also got to be a team player. Terry's strength at Chelsea has been organizing the defence and working with them to keep the goals out and keeping 'The Blues' on top.

Terry heads the ball during a training session for England in Germany, 2006.

John Terry is probably one of the most brilliant central defenders in the game. At Chelsea he has risen through the ranks to become captain. During the 2004/05 season he managed the defence supremely with Chelsea conceding just 15 goals – a record in football league history. Terry is well respected by footballers and fans – even rival London club Arsenal supporters! At 26 years old, the world is at his feet but he is a one-club man. He aims to stay with Chelsea until he hangs up his boots.

Terry is from a family of footballers. His father was a defender who regularly played on Sundays. While their dad played, Terry and his older brother kicked balls around at the sideline. Later, Terry played in the Sunday Football League, county football and was picked for West Ham schoolboys. Football was in his system. In those days, Terry played in midfield and that's where he wanted to stay. It wasn't until he made the Chelsea youth team that he switched to defence. Now he says that the feeling you get from saving a goal is as good as the high you get when scoring one.

At 17, Terry made his debut for the Chelsea first team. A stint with Nottingham Forest toughened up his act but in 2002 he hit the headlines. He was charged with assault at a London nightclub. Terry was acquitted but his reputation was tarnished for a while. He fought back and played better than ever. In 2003, he was chosen as captain for Chelsea. The same year, he made his debut for England. Chelsea won the league title in 2005 and 2006. Then, in 2006, Terry stepped into David Beckham's shoes to become captain of England. When he scored in a friendly against Greece in 2006 it looked like England had found a new golden boy.

> "John has all the attributes an international captain needs – leadership, authority, courage, ability, tactical awareness and a total refusal to accept second best… He has been an inspiration for Chelsea and is at his best in adversity."
>
> England coach Steve McClaren
> News.bbc.co.uk/sport

weblinks

For more information about John Terry, go to
www.waylinks.co.uk/21CentLives/Footballers

Michael Ballack
The Locomotive

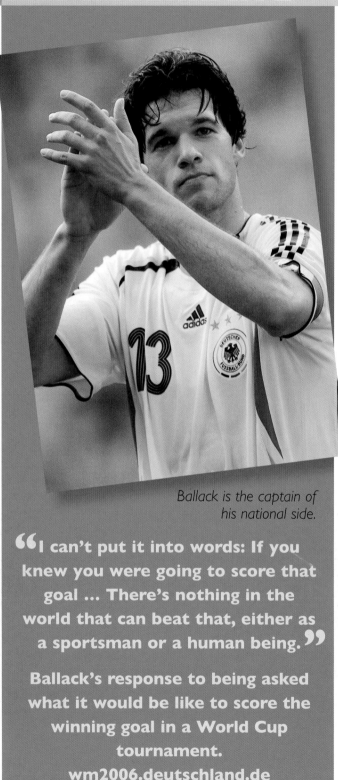

Ballack is the captain of his national side.

> **I can't put it into words: If you knew you were going to score that goal ... There's nothing in the world that can beat that, either as a sportsman or a human being.**

Ballack's response to being asked what it would be like to score the winning goal in a World Cup tournament.
wm2006.deutschland.de

Name: Michael Ballack

Nickname: Balle, Die Lokomotive, Little Kaiser

Current club and number: Chelsea FC, 13

Position: Midfielder

Date and place of birth:
26 September 1976, Görlitz, Saxony, Germany

First break: Ballack began training with the German club BSG Motor Karl-Marx-Stadt (now Chemnitz) when he was just seven years old.

Brief history: Ballack signed to Chemnitz, a second-division German club in 1995. The following year, he made his first appearance for Germany's Under-21 side. In 1997, Ballack moved into the *Bundesliga* (German premier division) when he signed to FC Kaiserslautern. He has since played for Bayer Leverkusen and the record-breaking German championship winners Bayern Munich. Then, in 2006, he switched to the English Premier League when he transferred to Chelsea FC. He made his debut for the German national side in 1999.

Major achievements: Being made captain of the German team in 2004. He's also bagged the German Player of the Year award three times (2002, 2003, 2005) and in 2006 he was chosen to play for his country's FIFA World Cup team.

Something you might not know about him: He passed his high school leaving exams and if his football career hadn't worked out he would have gone to university. He says he might even have followed his father into running an engineering firm.

Become a pro!: Ballack has a motto, which is not to take everything too seriously. He may be laid-back but the German midfielder is seriously good because of his flexibility. He can play at the back and the front of midfield, and he can play equally well with his left and right feet. Ballack is also known for his fantastic headers.

Michael Ballack is a footballing icon in his native Germany. The 'Little Kaiser' has an impressive strike rate – scoring 76 goals in nearly 240 league matches and 33 goals in 74 games for Germany.

Ballack was born in East Germany. When he was seven years old, he began training with Chemnitz. At the time his dream was to play for the East German first division. While his hopes were modest so were his opinions of himself. He never thought he would be captain of a squad and always looked to other players for the lead. Now he has played for the Bundesliga (the German Premier League) and the English Premier League, and he led his national team in the 2006 FIFA World Cup.

After two years with the first team at Chemnitz, Ballack transferred to Kaiserslautern in 1997. It was his first appearance in the *Bundesliga* and he truly made his mark. The club won the league title, becoming the first newly-promoted team in Germany ever to do so. In 1999 he shifted to Bayer Leverkusen and proved himself a strong all-rounder, capable of covering the entire pitch and scoring goals. In three seasons he scored 27 goals for the club. In 2001/02, Leverkusen reached the Champions League finals and came second in the *Bundesliga*. Ballack earned himself the title of German Player of the Year.

At the end of 2002, Ballack was at the top of his game and transferred to Bayern Munich. He helped to scoop three *Bundesliga* titles and German Cup doubles. Meanwhile, at the 2002 FIFA World Cup quarter and semi-finals Ballack stood out as Germany's star player. Unfortunately, a yellow card in the semi-final saw him miss out on the final against Brazil.

In 2006, Ballack was on the move again. This time to Stamford Bridge, home of 2006 Premier League champions, Chelsea FC. Since Russian billionaire Roman Abramovich took over the club in 2003 he has spent over £100 million buying a line-up of international football stars. Ballack is rumoured to be the highest-paid player in the English Premier League. He made his Chelsea debut in July 2006 and scored his first goal in September in a Champions League game against Werder Bremen.

Ballack at a pre-season friendly for Chelsea.

"He's one of the best players in the world. He's intelligent, tactically very strong and he scores a lot of goals. For me in Europe there's only Frank Lampard (Chelsea and England FC) who plays at that level. The two would form a dream pair."

Chelsea manager José Mourinho, before signing Ballack.
rediff.com/sports

weblinks

For more information about Michael Ballack, go to
www.waylinks.co.uk/21CentLives/Footballers

Cristiano Ronaldo
Soccer Sensation

Ronaldo smiles for the camera when he returns to the Manchester United squad in summer 2006.

"I would be very proud if, one day, I'm held in the same esteem as George Best or Beckham. It's what I'm working hard towards."

Cristiano Ronaldo
www.expertfootball.com

Name: Cristiano Ronaldo dos Santos Aveiro

Nickname: Ronnie

Current club and number:
Manchester United FC, 7

Position: Right winger/forward

Date and place of birth:
5 February 1985, Funchal, Madeira, Portugal

First break: Ronaldo kicked off for Madeira local youth team Andorinha when he was eight years old. He was soon snapped up to play for another local team, CD Nacional, where he became the star player. Ronaldo was a fan of the Portuguese team Sporting Lisbon. At 13 years old he was signed to the club and began training at the Alcochete, also known as the club's 'football factory'.

Brief history: When Ronaldo played for the Sporting Lisbon Under–18, Under–21 and first teams during one season, it was a club record. He made his debut for Portugal in August 2003, the same month that he signed a deal to play for Manchester United.

Major achievements: Becoming the most expensive teenager to sign to a British club. Manchester United made a deal for 18-year-old Ronaldo with Sporting Lisbon worth over £12 million. Another high for Ronaldo was scoring the 1000th Premiership goal for Manchester United in 2005.

Something you might not know about him: Ronaldo gave his support to victims of the Boxing Day tsunami of 2004. He visited Indonesia and raised money to help the survivors.

Become a pro!: Nifty and quick, Ronaldo has an array of enviable skills. He's an incredible crosser, passer and shooter. However, the young Portuguese player is known for his quick temper. Once he's mastered his moods he's tipped for the top!

Cristiano Ronaldo is one of the most gifted young players in the world today. He has youth and talent on his side. And, with his flair for flicks, tricks and step-overs he's a joy to watch.

Ronaldo's story is like a footballing fairytale. Born into a poor family on the Portuguese island of Madeira, he started playing football when he was three. His father was the kit man for the local amateur team Andorinha. It was here that Ronaldo's special talent grew. After a stint with local team Nacional, Ronaldo was pursued by major Portuguese clubs. He eventually signed to Sporting Lisbon schoolboys when he was just 13. It was a tough time for the island boy who was teased for his accent and he often got into fights. However, he could always prove himself on the pitch and scored two goals in his debut match for the first team.

Sir Alex Ferguson, manager of Manchester United, first spotted Ronaldo in a friendly match between Sporting Lisbon and Manchester United. Sporting beat United 3-1 and Ronaldo had set up two of the goals. In August 2003, Ronaldo, aged 18, was signed to Manchester United (the 'Red Devils'), becoming the most expensive teenager in Premiership history. Some people criticized Ferguson for paying so much for a player who had yet to prove himself. However, Ronaldo did not disappoint and in his debut against Bolton on 16 August 2003 he helped to set up two goals.

Fine performances for Portugal and Manchester United have kept Ronaldo at the top of the game. However, his time at United has been rocky. In 2005, in the space of a few months, he lost his father and was falsely accused of assault. Then, in the 2006 FIFA World Cup match between England and Portugal, Ronaldo complained about Wayne Rooney's foul against him to the referee. Rooney got a red card and England fans blamed Ronaldo for Rooney being sent off. Matters were made worse because Ronaldo and Rooney were team-mates at Manchester United. Throughout the summer of 2006 there was intense speculation that Ronaldo would sign to Real Madrid. Ronaldo decided to stay at Old Trafford. Recent performances have turned his reputation around and most fans have stopped booing him – many of them can be heard chanting, "there's only one Ronaldo!".

Ronaldo plays in a number 17 shirt for Portugal in the FIFA 2006 World Cup quarter-final.

> "If you just take the components – terrific physique, balance, pace, two feet – the potential [to become a top international player] is there."
>
> Sir Alex Ferguson, manager of Manchester United, during the run-up to Euro 2004.
> *Time* magazine, 13 June 2004

weblinks

For more information about Cristiano Ronaldo, go to
www.waylinks.co.uk/21CentLives/Footballers

Ronaldinho
The One Man Show

Ronaldhino is one of the most famous football players in the world.

> **God gives gifts to everyone. Some can write, some can dance. He gave me the skill to play football and I am making the most of it. I have always loved dribbling. I learned in my house, when I used to kick the ball against the wall and took on my dog in the garden, but this is a dream come true for me. When I see all the names on the list, my idols Ronaldo and Rivaldo, I realise this is a great honour.**

Ronaldinho on being chosen as 2005 European Player of the Year. The *Guardian*, 29 November 2005

Name: Ronaldo de Assis Moreira. He was christened Ronaldo but because there is another Brazilian called Ronaldo he is called Ronaldinho (Portuguese for 'Little Ronaldo').

Nickname: Ronaldinho Gaúcho, The One Man Show, Dinho, Ronnie

Current club and number: FC Barcelona, 10

Position: Forward/midfielder

Date and place of birth: 21 March 1980, Porto Alegre, Brazil

First break: In 1997, aged 17, Ronaldinho was chosen to play for his local youth club, Grêmio.

Brief history: In 1998, Ronaldinho played his first game for the Grêmio first team. The following year, he was selected for the Brazilian side. In 2001, he moved to France to play for Saint-Germain. He achieved star status when he scored two goals and helped Brazil on their way to winning the 2002 FIFA World Cup. The following year he moved to FC Barcelona in Spain.

Major achievements: In 2004, he was named FIFA World Player of the Year and World Soccer Player of the Year. In 2005, he won the same awards again and the FIFPro World Player of the Year, The European Footballer of the Year, World Soccer Player of the Year and the UEFA Champions League Most Valuable Player.

Something you might not know about him: His favourite film is Fernando Meirelle's *City of God*. The film is set in a Brazilian *favela* (slum, or shanty town). Ronaldhino claims that it is true-to-life and he should know, the first years of his life were spent in a *favela*.

Become a pro!: Ronaldhino says he tries to keep his game as simple as possible. Other players may not agree – he's well known for his no-look passes (also called blind passes) and football tricks.

Ronaldinho is one of the most talented players of his generation. His spectacular moves keep his opponents on their toes and the fans on the edge of their seats.

The story of Ronaldinho is a tale of rags to riches. He was born in Vila Nova, a poor neighbourhood in Porto Alegre in Brazil. Family was always important to him, as was music and football. His father was a shipyard worker who taught his young son valuable lessons about the game. As a boy Ronaldinho loved to dribble the ball. His father showed him how to touch the ball twice instead of dribbling. Ronaldo also learned his craft on the beach playing *futebol de salão*, an early version of *futsal* (five-a-side, indoor football), for two hours a night. The ball is smaller, heavier and less bouncy than a football. The game is played on a small pitch so ball control is vital. This is probably where Ronaldinho picked up his flair for quick manoeuvres and tricks.

Ronaldinho is known for his amazing tricks with the ball.

Ronaldinho first came to the media's attention when he was 13 and scored 23 goals in a local game. Soon afterwards he was signed to Grêmio. As his reputation grew, so did his football skills. He became well known for his blind passes, where he can aim a ball at a team-mate without even appearing to look. Skills like this did not go unnoticed and he was selected to play for Brazil's national team in 1999.

His next move was to Paris but this did not work out well. The young Brazilian missed home and seemed more interested in partying and staying out late. After

a dazzling display at the 2002 FIFA World Cup all eyes were back on Ronaldinho. Manchester United and Barcelona fought it out to sign the Brazilian. The move to Barcelona came in July 2003. It has been a golden opportunity for Ronaldinho. He has gone on to help his team win the 2004/05 and 2005/06 *La Liga* title and the 2006 UEFA Champions League. At the end of the 2005/06 season Ronaldinho had netted 25 goals – a personal best. Though his performance at the 2006 FIFA World Cup was disappointing, Ronaldinho still stands out as one of the finest players of all time.

"He is the most exquisite of footballers, his touch, his vision, his creativity, a genius you can safely put on the same planet with the likes of Maradona, Pelé, Johan Cruyff and [Franz] Beckenbauer. You don't even lump him with the merely great, wonderful players. What he does is not human."

Ray Hudson, ex-Miami Fusion coach
Miami Herald, 21 May 2006

weblinks

For more information about Ronaldinho, go to
www.waylinks.co.uk/21CentLives/Footballers

Andriy Shevchenko
The Eastern Wind

Shevchenko seems at home with his new club Chelsea.

" Lobanovsky was constantly looking ahead, trying to work out where football was going next. He was the first Ukrainian coach to use sports science to get the best out of his players... He taught me to be patient, he instilled the culture of work in me and the importance of respecting the adversary. He laid the foundations on which my career is based. **"**

Shevchenko talking about his coach at Dynamo, Valery Lobanovsky. The *Observer*, 3 September 2006.

Name: Andriy Mykolayovych Shevchenko

Nickname: Sheva, Shevagol, The Eastern Wind

Current club and number: Chelsea FC, 7

Position: Forward

Date and place of birth:
29, September 1976 Dvirkivschyna, Ukraine

First break: He was spotted by a scout for the Ukrainian team Dynamo Kyiv when he was ten. He joined the club's youth programme and remained with the junior team until 1994.

Brief history: He made his debut for Dynamo's first team in 1994. The following year, at just 19, he made his first appearance for his national side, Ukraine. In 1999, he signed for Italian club AC Milan where he became one of their top players. During the 2006 FIFA World Cup he was captain of the Ukrainian team and took them all the way to the quarter finals. In May 2006, he signed a deal with Chelsea FC.

Major achievements: Scoring the winning penalty for AC Milan in the final of the 2003 UEFA Champions League. In 2004, Shevchenko netted 24 league goals and Milan won the Scudetto title (another name for winning *Serie A*, the top division in Italian football). The same year, Shevchenko was named European Footballer of the Year. He's also the best scorer of all time in the history of the Champions League.

Something you might not know about him: He is friends with the fashion designer Giorgio Armani and has opened two boutiques with him in Kiev.

Become a pro!: Sheer ability to score goals, Shevchenko isn't scared to drive forward and get the ball in the net. He's disciplined, determined and an inspirational leader for the Ukrainian side.

Andriy Shevchenko is the most famous footballer to come from the Ukraine. At home he has superstar status. Now he has signed the record-breaking deal with Chelsea FC he is set to become a hero in the UK.

Shevchenko fights for the ball from Manchester City's Sylvain Distin.

Shevchenko was raised in Kiev, the capital of the Ukrainian Soviet Socialist Republic (now Ukraine). In 1986, the nuclear reactor at Chernobyl exploded. It was 60 miles away from Kiev and Shevchenko and his family were evacuated to the coast for a while. By now he was nine and showing promise on the pitch. Later that year he joined the Dynamo Kyiv youth team, based in Kiev. He travelled to Germany, Italy and England with the junior team. In 1990, he took part in the Ian Rush Cup in Wales and scooped the prize for top scorer of the tournament.

In 1994, Schevchenko made his debut for Dynamo. Dynamo Kyiv has taken part in Soviet and Ukrainian championships, and won both tournaments more than any other team. With Shevchenko on board they went on to win the league five times in five consecutive seasons (between 1994/95 and 1998/99). During 118 games he had scored 60 goals. Shevchenko's performances did not go unnoticed by foreign clubs and in 1999 he signed to AC Milan for £25 million. In his debut season he scored 24 league goals in 32 matches, making him the highest scorer in *Serie A*. In 2003, in the Champions League final between Milan and Juventus, Shevchenko scored the winning penalty. The following year he scored the winning goal in the UEFA Super Cup final between Milan and Porto.

Shevchenko was a key player in Milan's attack. In the summer of 2004, rumours of a transfer to Chelsea FC went down badly with the fans. At the time Shevchenko turned down offers to join Chelsea but in May 2006 he accepted a deal worth between £30 million and £56 million setting a record in the

English Premier League. The following month he was in Berlin at the FIFA World Cup leading his team into their first World Cup. Once again Shevchenko got the goals but it wasn't enough to take his team all the way. In August 2006, he was back in action in the English Premiership. A goal in his debut match for Chelsea against Liverpool was enough to send a shiver down anyone's back – 'The Eastern Wind' had arrived.

"He has great qualities, ambition, discipline, tactical awareness and of course he is a great goal scorer… He is a champion and he is joining a team of champions… Great players want to play with other great players."

Chelsea manager José Mourinho on Shevchenko moving to Chelsea FC.
BBC Sport, 31 May 2006
news.bbc.co.uk/sport1

weblinks

For more information about Andriy Shevchenko, go to
www.waylinks.co.uk/21CentLives/Footballers

Thierry Henry
Star Striker

Henry is sticking with Arsenal:
"This is my last contract. It is where I belong".

> **In five, six, seven years I'll be retired, and I want to be able to watch football on TV or attend a match and not hear a single racist insult... That's what I'd like to do for future generations of players. And that's what I'd like to give back to the game that has done so much for me.**
>
> **Thierry Henry**
> *Time*, **10 October 2005**

Name: Thierry Daniel Henry

Nickname: Titi, Terry, Tel, TH14

Current club and number: FC Barcelona, 14

Position: Forward

Date and place of birth:
17 August 1977, Paris, France

First break: As a schoolboy Henry played for his local youth team, Les Ulis. Later he played for the youth squads of Palaiseau, Viry-Châtillon and FC Versailles. At 17, Henry did a course at the French Football Federation's school at Clairefontaine.

Brief history: In 1994, Henry signed for AS Monaco. He made his debut for the French team in 1997 and in 1998 was the top goal scorer in his team at the FIFA World Cup. He was signed by Italian club Juventus in January 1999 but transferred to English Premier club Arsenal in September of the same year.

Major achievements: Henry is one of the most respected footballers in the game. He won the FWA Footballer of the Year award in 2003, 2004 and 2006, making him the only player to have scooped the title three times. He's won the PFA Player's Player of the Year and the European Golden Boot twice each. He has also been the FA Premier League top scorer four times.

Something you might not know about him: As a victim of football racism he started the Stand Up, Speak Up campaign with Nike. The charity raises money by selling black and white bracelets to football fans.

Become a pro!: Henry is fast, athletic and powerful. He's generous and plays more assists (the last completed pass from attacking player to goalscorer) than most. He has an instinct for scoring and has netted more goals for Arsenal than any other player.

Thierry Henry oozes talent and charisma. A sporting legend, he's the all-time third top goal scorer in the English Premiership and the second highest scorer of all time for France.

Born to Caribbean parents, Henry grew up in the Paris suburb, Les Ulis. It was a tough place but it has an excellent sports arena where Henry learned his football skills. Even though Henry wasn't naturally drawn to play football, his father encouraged him all the way. Henry had a gift for goal scoring, something that was picked up by a scout for AS Monaco who signed the boy when he saw him playing for youth football teams when he was just 13 years old. In 1994, Henry made his debut for AS Monaco. The manager, Arsène Wenger, placed him on the left wing. Henry performed well but it would be five years before he switched to attack and transformed into one of the most gifted strikers of all time.

Henry made his debut for France in 1997. During the 1998 FIFA World Cup he scored three goals and was the top scorer of the squad. This brought him into the international spotlight and in 1999 he transferred to Italian club Juventus. It was an unhappy time for Henry. He was placed on the wing and he lost his flair for scoring goals. A chance meeting with his ex-manager Arsène Wenger, who was now in charge of Arsenal, persuaded him to leave the club. In December 1999, Henry signed to Arsenal and Wenger placed him in the centre. He's never looked back. He's gone on to become the highest scorer of all time for Arsenal and in 2005 Wenger made him captain.

In May 2006, after months of speculation, Henry signed a new contract with Arsenal. The same month Arsenal players and fans said goodbye to their old stadium, Highbury. In the final game, Henry scored a hat-trick and kissed the pitch. It was one of many emotional and magical moments the Frenchman has shared with the club. More magic was to follow: in July 2006 Henry scored his first goal at the new Emirates Stadium.

Henry is so fast, he's been called a wizard with the ball.

"He terrorized them [Liverpool]. Afterwards, I spoke to a number of pros and they all said they hadn't seen anything like it. On his day, he had become unplayable, and more and more since then it has been his day. I have to say I haven't seen a player like him. He's an athlete with great technical ability and a tremendous desire to be the best."

Alan Smith, former Arsenal and England Striker
The *Observer*, 3 October 2004

Wayne Rooney

Young and gifted, Rooney is one of England's greatest football stars.

> **❝ I like to play with a little bit of temper. I think it makes my game better.... People say that nothing fazes me but I'm only a young lad and I promise you I get nervous before a game like anybody else. Everything I've done in my career has made the newspapers but my only concern is enjoying myself and getting a good experience.... ❞**
>
> **Wayne Rooney**
> **waynerooneyonline.com**

Name: Wayne Mark Rooney

Nickname: Wazza, Roonaldo

Current club and number:
Manchester United, 8

Position: Forward

Date and place of birth:
24 October 1985, Liverpool, England

First break: He kicked off at the age of seven with his local pub's under-12 side. Liverpool FC scouts had their eyes on him but it was Everton FC youth club that signed him up in 2000.

Brief history: At 16, Rooney made Everton's first team. In October 2002, in his debut match in the Premiership, he scored against Arsenal. Rooney made his first appearance for England in February 2003. In August 2004, after two seasons with Everton, Rooney was on the move to Manchester United.

Major achievements: Rooney is a sure-fire record-breaker. In 2003, at just 17, he became England's youngest player at that time when he played against Australia. Then, in the game against Macedonia later that year he became England's youngest goal scorer. In 2004, he became the youngest ever European at that time to score in the European Football Championships. He was winner of the PFA Young Player of the Year in 2005 and 2006, and the FIFPro Young Player of the Year in 2005.

Something you might not know about him: He raises money for Claire House and Alder Hey Children's hospitals in Liverpool. He is also an ambassador for the charity SOS Child.

Become a pro!: Do your own thing. A star striker needs to keep everyone guessing what he'll do next. With his speed, skill and power Rooney has all the right moves. He's as likely to run at defenders as well as take shots at goal from a distance.

Rooney plays in a number 9 shirt for England in the 2006 FIFA World Cup.

At Everton it became clear that Rooney was a star player. He was selected for the Under-19s side when he was only 15. In 2002, he was promoted to the first team. Later that year he made the headlines. He scored the winning goal against Arsenal in the last minute of a Premiership game. At just 16 years old, Rooney was the youngest goal scorer in the history of the Premiership. Early the next year, at the age of 17, Rooney made his debut for England. He broke another record to become the youngest player for the national team at that time. There was more to come. In October, in the European Championships qualifying match against Macedonia, he scored a goal and became England's youngest ever scorer. However, at the end of 2002 Rooney set the unfortunate record of being the youngest player ever to be sent off.

Rooney scored four goals for England at Euro 2004 and Manchester United were quick to sign him. In September 2004, in his debut for Manchester United against Fenerbahçe in the UEFA Champions League he struck a hat-trick. That season, he went on to score 11 goals in 29 league matches. In 2006, Rooney began to hit the headlines because of injury and failing to live up to the high expectations of fans and the media. Then, during the FIFA 2006 World Cup, he was sent off. By the end of 2006, Rooney had bounced back to form. A goal for England against the Netherlands put Rooney back in the news for all the right reasons.

'I have always said that Wayne Rooney is an amazing player, the kind of striker which any team in the world would like to have. He has the sort of forward's instinct, which you cannot buy and no coach can teach. You are born with it… He is someone who plays with absolutely no fear and when you have a striker like that then there are no limits. English football is very fortunate to have such a great striker.'

Thierry Henry, Arsenal striker, October 2004
waynerooneyonline.com

Wayne Rooney was just 18 when he scored two goals for England at Euro 2004. Since then he's rarely been out of the spotlight and is tipped to be the next Paul Gascoigne (Gazza). Why else has Rooney earned the nickname Wazza?

Rooney was raised in a working-class area of Liverpool called Croxteth. Born into a close-knit family that loves sport, Rooney showed early promise on the pitch. "He began to kick a ball as soon as he could walk," Rooney's father Wayne once said, "and he went to his first game when he was about six months old". The Rooneys are big Everton supporters and they were thrilled when young Rooney was spotted by a scout from the club when he was just nine-years-old.

weblinks

For more information about Wayne Rooney, go to
www.waylinks.co.uk/21CentLives/Footballers

Fabio Cannavaro
World Cup Hero

Cannavaro holds the World Cup close to him after Italy wins the tournament in 2006.

> **For an athlete it's as important how you behave off the pitch as you do on it ... Your body needs the right fuel to keep going. I don't smoke and I don't drink alcohol, I've never liked it. I live a normal, healthy life. I've been disciplined for many years and that has served me well.**
>
> **Fabio Cannavaro, 8 July 2006**
> **timesonline.co.uk**

Name: Fabio Cannavaro

Nickname: Il muro di Berlino (The Berlin Wall)

Current club and number: Real Madrid, 5

Position: Centre-back

Date and place of birth: 13 September 1973, Naples, Italy

First break: Spotted by talent scouts from his local club Napoli when he was just 16.

Brief history: Cannavaro made his debut in *Serie A* (equivalent to the Premier division in English football) for Napoli in 1993. He stayed with the club until 1995 when he signed for Parma FC. In 2002, he shifted to Inter Milan where he stayed for two years before joining Juventus. In 2006, after his legendary performance at the FIFA World Cup, he signed to Spanish club Real Madrid. He has played for the Italian national team since 1997.

Major achievements: Lifting the World Cup for Italy in July 2006. Many people agreed that Cannavaro was the man of the tournament but that accolade went to the French captain Zinedine Zidane who won the much-prized Golden Ball. Cannavaro won the Silver Ball. In 2005, Cannavaro picked up the *Oscar del Calcio* (awarded to the best players in the Italian Championship of Soccer).

Something you might not know about him: He has a fine array of tattoos, including the names of his sons Andrea and Christian and his wife Daniela. Also, look out for his tattoos of a warrior, the sun and Chinese characters.

Become a pro!: Cannavario is only 1.75 metres high but for what he lacks in height he makes up for in athleticism, speed and strength. He is also one of the most experienced international players and anticipates the ball well.

One of the lasting memories of the 2006 FIFA World Cup for Italians was captain Fabio Cannavaro raising the cup into the air. It was the first time Italy had won the cup in 24 years and Cannavaro's smile said it all. It was the highlight of his long and varied career.

As a boy Cannavaro played football before and after school. He even took his ball to bed with him. His favourite team was Napoli, and his heroes were Ciro Ferrara and Diega Maradona. In 1993, when he was 20, he made his debut for Napoli's first team against Juventus. Swift and gifted, Cannavaro was shaping up as a promising defender. However, a year later he was on the move to Italian club Parma. During his stay (1995–2002) Parma won two Italian Cups and the UEFA Cup. While he was at Parma, Cannavaro also made his debut in international football at the 1998 World Cup.

In 2002, Cannavaro joined Inter Milan. For a while he didn't perform well but a transfer to Juventus in 2004 was inspired. Cannavaro was back on form and Juventus won the league title in 2005. Meanwhile, Cannavaro was a rock solid presence in the Italian national team. He donned the famous blue strip for the 2002 World Cup and Euro 2004. After the 2002 World Cup, he was made captain of the Italian team. In 2006, Cannavaro was back at the World Cup, this time in Berlin, Germany. It was probably his last performance at a World Cup and he was determined to win: "We're going to have to sweat, scrap and suffer", he told reporters. In the final against France, Cannavaro made his one hundredth appearance for his country. France outplayed Italy but the Italians won on penalties. Many people felt Cannavaro had been the man of the tournament. He held together the Italian defence and never got a yellow or red card. The captain of the Italian team had been an example to everyone. The same could not be said of his home team, Juventus. In 2006, the club was relegated from *Serie A* for match-fixing. Soon after the victorious World Cup it was announced that Cannavaro was joining Real Madrid.

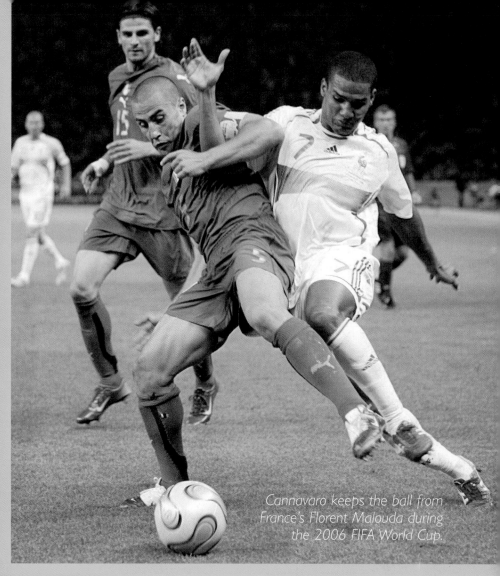

Cannavaro keeps the ball from France's Florent Malouda during the 2006 FIFA World Cup.

"He [Cannavaro] was everywhere the opposition didn't want him to be, [he] hoofed the ball well clear when the occasion demanded it, played it out with consummate ease when it didn't and even had a couple of chances on goal."

Georgina Turner of The *Guardian* on why she chose Cannavaro as the best player of 2006 FIFA World Cup.
The *Guardian*, 11 July 2006

weblinks

For more information about Fabio Cannavaro, go to
www.waylinks.co.uk/21CentLives/Footballers

Steven Gerrard
Midfield Powerhouse

Gerrard gets ready for England v. Ecuador in the 2006 FIFA World Cup.

"This caps a great weekend for me, what with getting through to the FA Cup Final and now winning this award. I was genuinely surprised and when you look at the names who have won the award in the past, it is an honour to be mentioned in the same breath as those people."

Steven Gerrard on being awarded the PFA Player of the Year Award for 2006, 24 April 2006.
liverpoolfc.tv/news

Name: Steven George Gerrard

Nickname: Stevie G

Current club and number: Liverpool FC, 8

Position: Midfielder

Date and place of birth:
30 May 1980, Whiston, England

First break: Played with Liverpool local youth team, Whiston Juniors. At nine years old he was spotted by scouts for Liverpool FC youth team.

Brief history: Gerrard was signed to Liverpool first team on 5 November 1997 but had to wait a year for his debut. He scored his first goal for Liverpool against Sheffield Wednesday in December 1999. On 31 May 2000, Gerrard was called up to play for England. In 2003, he was appointed captain of Liverpool and in 2006 he was named vice-captain of England.

Major achievements: As well as being captain for Liverpool and vice-captain for England, Gerrard has won 2001 PFA Young Player of the Year, 2004/05 UEFA Champions League Most Valuable Player and 2006 PFA Player of the Year.

Something you might not know about him: In 2006, Gerrard published his autobiography. It had good reviews because it was a good read for real soccer fans, interested in how he grew up and got into the game, his thoughts and feelings about the game and its leading characters.

Become a pro!: As well as having great leadership skills it helps if you have boundless energy and the ability to cover the pitch. Gerrard is a great team player who can make crucial passes and block the most deadly attack. He can also turn on the magic and score brilliant goals.

Steven Gerrard is the only England player to have scored in four major cup finals. He won the 2006 PFA Player of the Year and is now vice-captain for England.

Gerrard was born and raised in Merseyside. Football is in his blood. His father was a notable amateur player and his cousin played for Everton. Gerrard was a Liverpool fan and always hoped to join their ranks. When he was nine he was picked for the Liverpool youth team. Small for his age, and a slow starter, he only managed 20 matches between the ages of 14 and 16. At 14, he had a trial for Manchester United but all he wanted was to play for Liverpool. He hoped he'd get to play with his friend Michael Owen (see page 22), the ex-Liverpool striker. He reckoned they would make a great partnership with Gerrard setting up the goals for Owen. In 1997, aged 17, Gerrard finally signed to Liverpool.

In the 2000/01 season, Liverpool won the treble cup: the League Cup, the FA Cup and the UEFA Cup. Gerrard scored in the UEFA Cup final. In 2000, he made his debut for England against Ukraine. He went on to score for England in the 2001 World Cup qualifying game against Germany. Gerrard is one of the best midfielders of his generation. A great all-rounder, he is famous for his staying power, ability to set up passes, score goals and remain focused when the odds are against him. The year ended on a high with Gerrard being awarded the 2001 PFA Young Player of the Year Award.

In 2003/04, Gerrard became captain of Liverpool. Liverpool was runner-up in the 2004/05 Premier League Cup and it looked like Gerrard might leave Liverpool for London club, Chelsea. It was a nail-biting time for fans and Gerrard, who had once claimed he'd never leave Anfield. Gerrard's goal against AC Milan in the final of the 2005 Champions League kept Liverpool in the game. Liverpool went on to win the cup and Gerrard told reporters he would be staying with the club. It's a promise he's kept and in 2005/06 he scored 23 goals for the club. The same year he lifted up the FA Cup for Liverpool. Any suggestions that he might leave Liverpool are batted away: "I'll be staying here until the day someone tells me they don't want me".

Gerrard is a great all-round player. He was nearly made into a striker for the 2006 FIFA World Cup.

"If you want to look for a perfect footballer just look at Steven Gerrard He's got great athleticism, he's quick. In fact, he's just about got everything. He could play in any position and do it well."

Michael Owen, The *Independent*
28 May 2006

weblinks

For more information about Steven Gerrard, go to
www.waylinks.co.uk/21CentLives/Footballers

Other Footballers

Damian Duff

Irish winger Damian Duff was born on 2 March 1979 in Ballyboden, Dublin in the Republic of Ireland. His career kicked off in 1996 when he joined Blackburn Rovers. By 1998, he was playing for Ireland. Best on the left, Duff is still good enough to play on either side. He's quick and gives one hundred per cent. In his six years with Blackburn Rovers he made 185 appearances and scored 27 goals. In 2001, he was part of the winning line-up that saw Blackburn promoted to the Premier division. In 2002, Blackburn won the League Cup and major clubs such as Chelsea FC, showed interest in him. In July 2003, Duff signed a transfer deal with Chelsea. His early days at Chelsea were marred by injury but he returned to form and scored ten goals in the 2004/05 season. The next season was disappointing and Duff was on the move again. Tottenham Hotspur and Liverpool were hot on his trail but in July 2006 Duff signed a five-year contract with Newcastle United. On 17 September 2006, he scored his first goal for 'The Magpies' at Newcastle.

Ryan Giggs

Ryan Joseph Gigggs, also known as the 'Welsh Wizard' or 'Giggsy', was born in Cardiff on 29 November 1973. He plays left wing or centre midfield and is the captain of Wales, for whom he has scored eleven goals. However, it is his successful and long-lasting career with Premiership club Manchester United for which he is most famous. He is vice-captain of Manchester United and is the longest serving player in the current team. Among his many achievements, he holds the record for scoring the most goals by a player not in the position of striker in the Premier League. Awards include the PFA Young Player of the Year for 1992 and 1993 and the Manchester United Player's Player

of the Year for 2005/2006. His career began when he signed to Manchester City youth team at just 14. Manchester United manager Alex Ferguson was keen to sign the promising new winger and, in 1991, Giggs made his debut for 'The Reds'. The following year Giggs was in the Welsh squad. Early in his career, his good looks turned him into a pin-up but it was his speed and dribbling skills on the pitch that earned him the title 'Boy Wonder'. Giggs remains a key player for United and has become a role model for younger team-mates like Wayne Rooney (see pages 16-17).

Michael Owen

Born in Chester, England, Michael James Owen, also known as 'Saint Michael', is a forward for England and Newcastle United. As a schoolboy, Owen was already looking hot on the pitch and breaking goal scoring records. In 1991, after major teams such as Manchester United, Chelsea FC and Arsenal had shown an interest, Owen signed to the Liverpool FC youth team. Owen was a life-long Everton fan but it was with rivals Liverpool that he shot to fame.

In 1996, aged 17, he made his debut for the first team. In his stunning 1997/98 season, he scored 18 goals to become the joint top scorer of the Premier League. The same year, he made his debut for England. At the 1998 World Cup, he was pulled off the sub bench to score a goal against Romania. Then, during the second round, in the match against Argentina, he scored an unforgettable goal. The year ended on a bigger high when he was awarded the PFA Young Player of the Year award. Owen stayed with Liverpool until 2004 when he was signed by Real Madrid. The following season, Owen moved back to England and signed for Newcastle United. A hat-trick against West Ham United in December 2005 heralded a return to form but unfortunately injuries kept him away for most of the season. Owen is regarded as one of England's top strikers. He's appeared in three World Cups and has scored 36 goals for his country, making him the fourth top scorer for England of all time.

David Beckham

'Becks', 'Goldenballs', 'DB7', call him what you like, but David Beckham has lived the dream to become an icon of the sporting world. He was born on 2 May 1975 in Leytonstone in London, England. His own dream was to play for Manchester United. In 1991, aged thirteen, he was signed up for United's youth team. In 1995, he made his debut for the first team and, in 1996, he caught the public's eye when he scored a stunning goal against Wimbledon from the halfway line. The same year he made his debut for England and won the PFA Young Player of the Year award. In the 1998 World Cup, he was sent off during the match against Argentina. Many people blamed him for England going out of the Cup. At home, Beckham was hounded by the press but he bounced back and in 1999 Manchester United won the treble: the League, the FA Cup and Champions League. In 2000, he was made captain of England and at the 2002 FIFA World Cup he fought back from injury to score against arch rivals, Argentina.

For years Beckham braved the dispute between himself and manager Alex Ferguson. However, in 2003, he waved goodbye to Ferguson and United and signed a deal with Spanish club Real Madrid. Away from England, but never far away from the British newspapers, Beckham remains a household name. He was captain of the England squad for the 2006 FIFA World Cup but despite his solid performances he decided to stand down as captain after the tournament. In August 2006, Beckham was dropped from the England side – it was the end of an era. But in May 2007, after playing well for Real Madrid, David was recalled to the England Squad.

Peter Crouch

Peter James Crouch, affectionately known as Crouchy, was born in Macclesfield, England on 30 January 1981. He was signed to Tottenham in 1998 and played for the youth team. His professional teams include Queen's Park Rangers (2000–2001), Portsmouth (2001–2002), Aston Villa (2002–2004), Norwich City (2003), Southampton (2004–2005) and Liverpool (2005–present). He made his debut for England in 2005 against Colombia. In a friendly against Jamaica, in June 2006, he scored a hat-trick.

It must be hard to live down the nickname 'Two Metre Peter' or even *La Jirafa* ('The Giraffe' – so called because he's a whopping 2.01 metres tall) as he is known in Spanish, but England striker Peter Crouch is fast becoming an unlikely hero. Part of his status is down to his performance at the 2006 FIFA World Cup when at times he looked like England's only hope of a goal. However, after the World Cup Crouch really found his feet, scoring two goals in a friendly match against Greece and two goals in a qualifying match for Euro 2008 against Andorra. His run of goals has earned him the record of being the first England player to score ten goals within a year. To cap these fine performances Crouch was potting goals for Liverpool FC. At the beginning of the 2006/07 season, he scored the winning goal against Chelsea in the FA Community Shield and then, in September 2006, he made two spectacular goals against Galatasaray in the UEFA Champions League.

Index

21st Century Lives

Contents of all books in the series: